PROPERTY OF
**CUYAHOGA COUNTY
PUBLIC LIBRARY**
2111 Snow Road
Parma, Ohio 44134

OHIO

A MyReportLinks.com Book

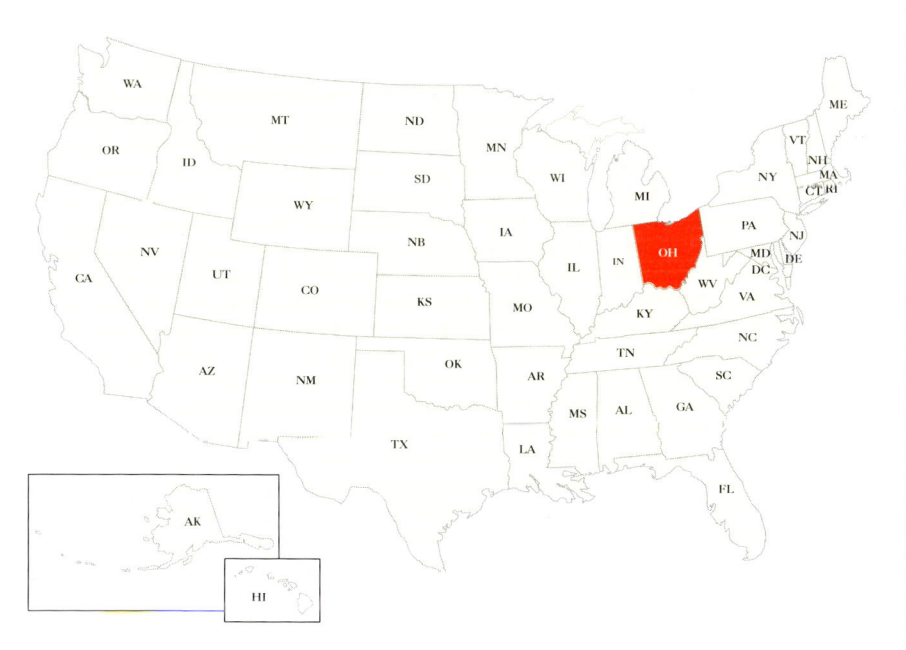

Ron Knapp

MyReportLinks.com Books
an imprint of
Enslow Publishers, Inc.
Box 398, 40 Industrial Road
Berkeley Heights, NJ 07922
USA

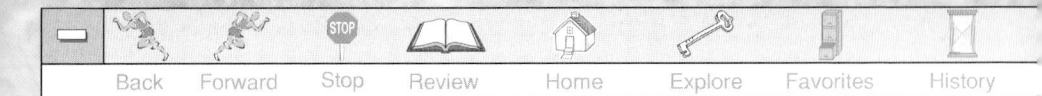

For Neil and Diane Croften, Buckeye runners

MyReportLinks.com Books, an imprint of Enslow Publishers, Inc. MyReportLinks is a trademark of Enslow Publishers, Inc.

Copyright © 2002 by Enslow Publishers, Inc.

All rights reserved.

No part of this book may be reproduced by any means without the written permission of the publisher.

Library of Congress Cataloging-in-Publication Data

Knapp, Ron.
 Ohio / Ron Knapp.
   p. cm. — (States)
 Summary: Discusses the land and climate, economy, government, and history of the Buckeye State. Includes Internet links to Web sites, source documents, and photographs related to Ohio.
 Includes bibliographical references and index.
   ISBN 0-7660-5022-X
   1. Ohio—Juvenile literature. [1. Ohio.] I. Title. II. States (Series: Berkeley Heights, N.J.)
 F491.3 .K48 2002
 977.1—dc21
                             2001008190

Printed in the United States of America

10 9 8 7 6 5 4 3 2 1

To Our Readers:
Through the purchase of this book, you and your library gain access to the Report Links that specifically back up this book.
 The Publisher will provide access to the Report Links that back up this book and will keep these Report Links up to date on www.myreportlinks.com for three years from the book's first publication date.
 We have done our best to make sure all Internet addresses in this book were active and appropriate when we went to press. However, the author and the Publisher have no control over, and assume no liability for, the material available on those Internet sites or on other Web sites they may link to.
 The usage of the MyReportLinks.com Books Web site is subject to the terms and conditions stated on the Usage Policy Statement on **www.myreportlinks.com**.
 In the future, a password may be required to access the Report Links that back up this book. The password is found on the bottom of page 4 of this book.
 Any comments or suggestions can be sent by e-mail to comments@myreportlinks.com or to the address on the back cover.

Photo Credits: American Destinations Digital Stock, p. 44; © 1998 Corbis Corp. Digital Stock, p. 44; © Corel Corporation, p. 3, 10 (flag); 1-800-BUCKEYE www.OhioTourism.com, pp. 13, 17, 19, 34, 39; *Dictionary of American Portraits*, Dover Publications, Inc., © 1967, p. 42; Enslow Publishers, Inc., p. 1 (map), 16; Knorek.com, p. 41; Library of Congress, p. 27; MyReportLinks.com Books, p. 4; National Archives, p. 42; Ohio Biography, p. 29; Ohio History Central, p. 36; Ohio.gov, p. 32; President Benjamin Harrison Home, p. 25; Thinkquest Library, p. 37; Time magazine, p. 23; Toledo Zoo, p. 14; University of Dayton, p. 21

Cover Photo: 1-800-BUCKEYE www.OhioTourism.com

Cover Description: Rock and Roll Hall of Fame and Museum

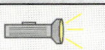

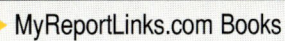

Contents

    Report Links **4**

    Ohio Facts **10**

1 **The Buckeye State** **11**

2 **Land and Climate** **16**

3 **Famous Ohioans** **20**

4 **Government and Economy** **32**

5 **History** **35**

    Chapter Notes **46**

    Further Reading **47**

    Index **48**

Back　Forward　Stop　Review　Home　Explore　Favorites　History

About MyReportLinks.com Books

MyReportLinks.com Books
Great Books, Great Links, Great for Research!

MyReportLinks.com Books present the information you need to learn about your report subject. In addition, they show you where to go on the Internet for more information. The pre-evaluated Report Links that back up this book are kept up to date on **www.myreportlinks.com**. With the purchase of a MyReportLinks.com Books title, you and your library gain access to the Report Links that specifically back up that book. The Report Links save hours of research time and link to dozens—even hundreds—of Web sites, source documents, and photos related to your report topic.

Please see "To Our Readers" on the Copyright page for important information about this book, the MyReportLinks.com Books Web site, and the Report Links that back up this book.

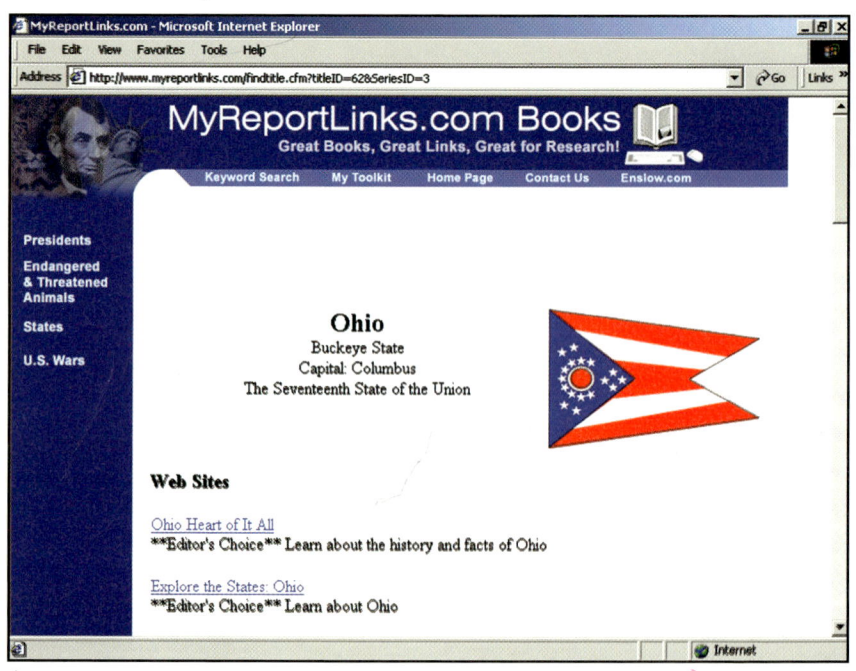

Access:

The Publisher will provide access to the Report Links that back up this book and will try to keep these Report Links up to date on our Web site for three years from the book's first publication date. Please enter **SOH1768** if asked for a password.

4

| Tools | Search | Notes | Discuss | ▶ MyReportLinks.com Books | Go! |

Report Links

The Internet sites described below can be accessed at http://www.myreportlinks.com

*EDITOR'S CHOICE

▶Ohio: Heart of It All
This site provides information about Ohio, including the state flower, a picture of the flag, and a listing of the birthplaces of seven United States presidents. There are links from each topic to find out more information.

Link to this Internet site from http://www.myreportlinks.com

*EDITOR'S CHOICE

▶Explore the States: Ohio
America's Story from America's Library, a Library of Congress Web site, provides information about Ohio, which was admitted to the Union in 1803. There are links to "more stories about Ohio," such as the Historic Sauder Village, which reenacts the way people lived in Ohio in the 1830s.

Link to this Internet site from http://www.myreportlinks.com

*EDITOR'S CHOICE

▶Ohio's History Central
At this Web site you will find information about Ohio's nature, prehistoric history, and American Indian heritage.

Link to this Internet site from http://www.myreportlinks.com

*EDITOR'S CHOICE

▶Ohio Presidents
At this Web site you will find brief biographies of eight United States presidents from Ohio. You will also find links to more information about each president.

Link to this Internet site from http://www.myreportlinks.com

*EDITOR'S CHOICE

▶Ohio Historical Society
This site contains lots of information about Ohio's history, including photographs, information about the African-American experience in Ohio, Civil War documents, and a link created by Ohio Kids that has games and fun facts.

Link to this Internet site from http://www.myreportlinks.com

*EDITOR'S CHOICE

▶State of Ohio Government
This comprehensive site has information about Ohio's communities, cultural events, businesses, education, tourism, and government.

Link to this Internet site from http://www.myreportlinks.com

Any comments? Contact us: comments@myreportlinks.com

Report Links

The Internet sites described below can be accessed at http://www.myreportlinks.com

▶**City of Columbus, Ohio**
This site about Columbus, Ohio, gives a detailed history of the city with news, information, and happenings. It also provides many photographs and links.

Link to this Internet site from http://www.myreportlinks.com

▶**Explorers of the Millennium**
This brief site contains information about René-Robert Cavelier, one of the first white people to visit the Ohio Valley. The site also contains links to other places to learn about Cavelier.

Link to this Internet site from http://www.myreportlinks.com

▶**Friends of Freedom Society**
This Web site lists information about how to research the Underground Railroad in Ohio, and has links to historic homes that participated in the Underground Railroad. There is also a link to the Hubbard House museum, which has photos of exhibitions and historic artifacts.

Link to this Internet site from http://www.myreportlinks.com

▶**Harriet Beecher Stowe Biography**
Harriet Beecher Stowe lived in Cincinnati and housed fugitive slaves there in the 1850s. This site gives a biographical sketch of her life, and has links to other sources.

Link to this Internet site from http://www.myreportlinks.com

▶**Official Jesse Owens Site**
At this site you can learn about the life of this incredible athlete. There are photos of Jesse Owens, personal quotes, and a list of his achievements.

Link to this Internet site from http://www.myreportlinks.com

▶**Ohio**
At this site you can find out about the history of the Ohio River, how floods and canals are controlled, and the impact humans have on the river.

Link to this Internet site from http://www.myreportlinks.com

Any comments? Contact us: **comments@myreportlinks.com**

MyReportLinks.com Books

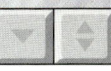

Tools   Search   Notes   Discuss   Go!

Report Links

The Internet sites described below can be accessed at
http://www.myreportlinks.com

▶ **Ohio Arts Council**
This site contains information about funding for the arts in Ohio, including photos of art exhibits, information about upcoming art festivals, and workshops for children and adults.

Link to this Internet site from http://www.myreportlinks.com

▶ **The Ohio Bicentennial**
In 2003, Ohio will celebrate its two hundredth anniversary. This site documents the programs and activities that will take place, including the bronzing of eighty-eight bells which will be placed in each county in Ohio.

Link to this Internet site from http://www.myreportlinks.com

▶ **Ohio Biography**
This site has brief biographical information about prominent Ohio natives, including Toni Morrison, James Thurber, John Glenn, and more. Each biography includes a photograph and links to related Web sites.

Link to this Internet site from http://www.myreportlinks.com

▶ **Ohio Department of Natural Resources**
Explore information about Ohio's parks, reserves, scenic lakes, and wildlife. This site also contains links to lists of rare plants, photos of different bird species, and a link to a live "birdwatcher cam" that changes pictures of birds feeding every three minutes.

Link to this Internet site from http://www.myreportlinks.com

▶ **Ohio Railroads**
At this site you can read about the history of Ohio's railroads, and see photos of old maps and trains. There are also pages about where to go and see trains today.

Link to this Internet site from http://www.myreportlinks.com

▶ **The Ohio Senate**
This informative site contains pages that outline the history of Ohio's state senate, and explain how the senate works. There is also an interactive map that you can click on to see which senators serve in each district.

Link to this Internet site from http://www.myreportlinks.com

Any comments? Contact us: comments@myreportlinks.com

Back Forward Stop Review Home Explore Favorites History

Report Links

The Internet sites described below can be accessed at
http://www.myreportlinks.com

▶ **Ohio State Buckeyes**
This site contains photos of the football and basketball teams at Ohio State with live audio visual links, and includes the history of the Buckeye mascot.

Link to this Internet site from http://www.myreportlinks.com

▶ **Ohio State Library**
This site has information about the history of the Ohio State Library, a searchable online catalog of the state library's materials, and links to all the public libraries in Ohio.

Link to this Internet site from http://www.myreportlinks.com

▶ **Ohio Tourism**
This site contains tips about where to stay in Ohio, recreational activities, an events calendar, and a searchable database of attractions.

Link to this Internet site from http://www.myreportlinks.com

▶ **Paul Laurence Dunbar**
This resourceful site includes a biography of Paul Dunbar's life, a collection of his poetry, pages of essays about his work, photos of his birthplace, and many additional links.

Link to this Internet site from http://www.myreportlinks.com

▶ **Prehistoric Ohio**
This Web site contains information about Ohio's soil today and also the geology and fossilized remains from prehistoric Ohio. There are links to sites with information on different time periods, such as the Cretaceous and Cambrian eras.

Link to this Internet site from http://www.myreportlinks.com

▶ **Rivers Unleashed**
This interesting site is dedicated to the various floods that have plagued Ohio throughout the years. There are quotes, historic accounts of floods, and photos of Ohio being flooded in 1937.

Link to this Internet site from http://www.myreportlinks.com

Any comments? Contact us: comments@myreportlinks.com

MyReportLinks.com Books

Tools   Search   Notes   Discuss   Go!

Report Links

➤ The Internet sites described below can be accessed at
http://www.myreportlinks.com

▶ **Stately Knowledge: Ohio**
This concise Web site lists basic facts about Ohio, but also contains links to encyclopedias and almanacs that have more extensive information about Ohio.

Link to this Internet site from http://www.myreportlinks.com

▶ **Time 100 Scientists: The Wright Brothers**
This information packed site has an essay about the Wright brothers, as well as a photographic slide show, movie clip of their flying skills, and link to their national memorial.

Link to this Internet site from http://www.myreportlinks.com

▶ **Today In History**
At this Web site you will learn how on February 28, 1827, the Baltimore and Ohio Railroad became the first railway for commercial and passenger use.

Link to this Internet site from http://www.myreportlinks.com

▶ **Toledo Zoo**
You can navigate through the zoo using an interactive map by clicking on different animals and learning about them. There are also trivia questions, an "animal cam," and a kid's corner with games.

Link to this Internet site from http://www.myreportlinks.com

▶ **United States Air Force Museum**
This site has photos of a variety of weapons and aircrafts on display at the museum, including pictures of the presidential airplanes. There are also links to archives, space flight crafts, historic uniforms, and current exhibitions.

Link to this Internet site from http://www.myreportlinks.com

▶ **Victoria Woodhull**
Ohio native Victoria Woodhull was the first woman to run for president. This site has a biographical time line of her life and links to essays and other resources.

Link to this Internet site from http://www.myreportlinks.com

Any comments? Contact us: comments@myreportlinks.com   9

Ohio Facts

▶ **Capital**
Columbus

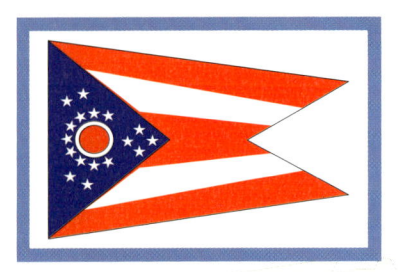

▶ **Population**
11,353,140*

▶ **Gained Statehood**
March 1, 1803

▶ **State Bird**
Cardinal

▶ **State Tree**
Buckeye

▶ **State Flower**
Scarlet carnation

▶ **State Animal**
White-tailed deer

▶ **Gemstone**
Ohio flint

▶ **Song**
"Beautiful Ohio," words by Ballard MacDonald, music by Mary Earl.

▶ **Motto**
With God, all things are possible.

▶ **Flag**
Adopted in 1902; the triangle represents Ohio's hills and valleys, and the stripes symbolize roads and waterways. The seventeen stars signify Ohio as the seventeenth state. The white circle with a red center stands for an O for Ohio, as well as the buckeye nut.[1]

▶ **State Seal**
The seal, adopted in 1967, bears a sheaf of wheat and a bundle of seventeen arrows for the seventeenth state. The wheat represents Ohio's strong agriculture. The thirteen rays of sun represent the original thirteen colonies shining over the state. In the background is Mount Logan, signifying that Ohio was the first state west of the Allegheny Mountains.[2]

▶ **Nickname**
Buckeye State

*Population reflects the 2000 census.

Chapter 1 ▶

The Buckeye State

You can tell a lot about Ohio just by looking at its flag. Unlike the flags of the other forty-nine states, Ohio's flag is tapered and pointed. Like the national flag, its only colors are red, white, and blue.

The stripes represent the many roads and waterways that crisscross the state. The big blue triangle stands for Ohio's hills and valleys. The seventeen stars are a reminder that Ohio was the seventeenth state admitted to the Union.

The white circle, of course, stands for the first letter in the state's name. The middle red circle represents the buckeye nut. When American settlers first came to the area, it was covered by big buckeye trees. Thousands of them were cut down and used to make log cabins.

The people of Ohio have never forgotten the tree that gave them their first houses. The nickname of Ohio, after almost two hundred years, remains "The Buckeye State," and athletic teams from Ohio State University are known as the Buckeyes.

▶ Something Great

Before white settlers arrived, the land that would become Ohio was populated by the Iroquois Indians. They used the long, wide river there as a highway. It was so important to them that they called it "ohio," or something great. The new settlers kept the name for the river and eventually called their state by the same name. Today the Ohio River forms the border between the state and Kentucky and West Virginia.

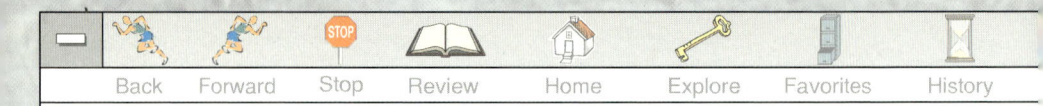

Ohio has a fascinating history. No fewer than eight presidents were born or lived there. Its factories and farms have been productive. Ohio's colleges have a proud athletic tradition. The state is home to professional sports teams such as the Bengals and Reds in Cincinnati and the Browns, Cavaliers, and Indians in Cleveland. There is a professional hockey team in the state, the Columbus Blue Jackets, as well as pro soccer and women's basketball teams.

▶ Sports and Competitions

Ohio's major cities are home to some of the nation's most popular sports teams. Almost 100,000 football fans regularly fill Ohio Stadium in Columbus to cheer for the Ohio State Buckeyes. The National Hockey League's Blue Jackets are in Columbus as well. Beautiful Jacobs Field is home to baseball's Cleveland Indians. The Reds, another Major League Baseball team, play in Cincinnati.

The Cleveland Browns and Cincinnati Bengals compete in the National Football League. The Cleveland Cavaliers play in the National Basketball Association.

The Pro Football Hall of Fame is located in Canton, which had been the home of one of professional football's first teams, the Bulldogs. Displays celebrate the history of the National Football League and the leagues that came before it.

You do not have to be a professional runner to compete in the Columbus Marathon. It is a 26.2-mile footrace through the streets of the city. Some big-city marathons require minimum qualifying times, but not Columbus. Anybody brave enough to try is welcome. If a runner cannot make it the whole way, a three-person relay team can split the distance.

The All-American Soap Box Derby, where kids race their homemade cars down a hill, has been a summer highlight in Akron since 1934. They qualify for the big race by winning one of the dozens of regional events around the country. Winners get college scholarships and other prizes.

▶ Museums to Visit

The United States Air Force Museum, one of the world's greatest aviation museums, is located in Dayton. It displays more than three hundred full-sized planes. Bombers, fighter planes, commercial jets, and missiles can be viewed inside hangers or on the runways. One of the most popular exhibits is President John F. Kennedy's *Air Force One*, the plane that flew his body back to Washington, D.C., after his assassination.

▲ Jacobs Field, located in Cleveland, is home to the Cleveland Indians.

The Health Museum of Cleveland features information on the way human bodies work and how to keep them healthy. Cleveland is also the home of the Rock and Roll Hall of Fame and Museum. Visitors can see plaques honoring popular singers and musicians. Videos and documentary films are shown constantly. Rock artifacts such as costumes worn by Elvis Presley, the Beatles, and Madonna are displayed.

▶ Fun in Ohio

Some of the country's great zoos are in Ohio. The Toledo Zoo is famous for its Hippoaquarium, a giant

▲ Tourists flock to the Toledo Zoo to catch a glimpse of a family of hippopotamuses in the zoo's famous Hippoaquarium.

aquarium for a family of hippopotamuses. The Cleveland Metroparks Zoo has an African Plains Savanna for zebras and giraffes, and an Australian Adventure featuring kangaroos and koalas. The Rainforest features more than six hundred animals from all over the world.

Rare white Bengal tigers and an underwater polar bear viewing area are highlights at the Cincinnati Zoo. The Wilds, near Cumberland, is the nation's largest wildlife preserve and research facility. Endangered animals such as white rhinos are cared for there.

Cedar Point Amusement Park in Sandusky has more roller coasters than any other park in the world. One ride called "Millennium Force" zips riders down a 310-foot drop at more than ninety miles an hour.

Six Flags Ohio in Aurora features rides such as Batman Knight Flight and Superman Ultimate Escape. Paramount's Kings Island features Drop Zone and the Beast, one of the world's longest wooden roller coasters.

Chapter 2

Land and Climate

For thousands of years, most of North America was covered with ice. As the earth cooled, giant glaciers pushed southward from the Arctic region. Loose stones were bulldozed ahead of the creeping glaciers. Hills were leveled. Giant holes were scraped out of the land. The ice was two miles thick in some places. It was the last great Ice Age.

About ten thousand years ago, temperatures began to rise. The glaciers melted, filling the big holes with water

▲ Map of Ohio.

and leaving a huge plain. That is why today Ohio is a flat state. The only good-sized hills are in the southern part of the state in places where the glaciers never reached.

The big holes became the Great Lakes. The smallest one, Lake Erie, got its name from the Iroquois. Lake Erie separates Ohio from the Canadian border.

Of course, Ohio has plenty of other water. One of North America's biggest rivers, the Ohio River, forms 450 miles of the state's southern border. There are more than 44,000 miles of streams and rivers in Ohio, and the state also has 2,500 large lakes.

▲ *Columbus is Ohio's largest city and state capital.*

The Ice Age is over, but the northern regions of Ohio still get plenty of snow and cold weather in the winter. The state's average temperature in January is 28°F. Summers are warm and humid with an average July temperature of 73°F.

▶ Ohio's Cities

Ohio's four largest cities stretch from the Ohio River to Lake Erie. The largest is Columbus, which is located in the middle of the state. It is the state capital and home of the main campus of Ohio State University. Many research agencies and computer information businesses are based in Columbus.

Cleveland, situated on Lake Erie, is known for manufacturing and shipping. Cincinnati's riverfront location along the Ohio River makes it one of the prettiest cities in America. Toledo, built on the spot where the Maumee River meets Lake Erie, is also an important port.

▶ Disaster in Dayton

A heavy rainfall in the spring of 1913 caused the Miami River to overflow its banks. The floods turned deadly when the rains kept coming. Homes and businesses were washed away. Dayton was almost destroyed.

Approximately 350 people were killed by the floods, which caused more than $100 million in damage. The people of Dayton began the long process of rebuilding their city and the state took steps to make sure the disaster would not reoccur.

Plans were made to control an entire river for the first time in history. Dams, reservoirs, levees, and floodgates were built along the length of the Miami River. The project cost millions of dollars, but it was successful. Since then, many other communities have copied the Miami River project.

▶ Natural Tourist Attractions

Most of Ohio is not amusement parks or big cities. About a quarter of the state's land is covered by forests. There are hundreds of small towns, and thousands of farms line the country roads.

Historic Lyme Village in Bellevue, Zoar Village near Canton, and Schoenbrunn Village near New Philadelphia have displays of buildings and crafts that demonstrate how Ohio's early white settlers lived.

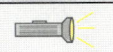

One of the state's most interesting tourist attractions was one of the first things built there by humans. The Adena Indians used baskets of dirt to make a long mound in the shape of a snake. The Great Serpent Mound, located near Locust Grove, is five feet high and 1,300 feet long. Trapped in its huge jaws is something that looks like a giant egg that is thirty feet wide.

Mound Builders Earthworks, in Newark, and Hopewell Culture National Historic Park, near Chillicothe, preserve examples of mounds constructed by the Hopewell Indians.

Ohio Caverns, near West Liberty, is famous for its beautifully colored walls. Its stalactites and stalagmites, however, are pure white. They are the largest limestone caves in the state.

▲ *Ohio Caverns, located near West Liberty, is famous for its colorful walls and pure white stalagmites and stalactites.*

Chapter 3

Famous Ohioans

Ohio has produced some of the most unique characters in American history. They have made their mark in many fields, but especially in politics and sports.

▶ Young Poet

Matilda Dunbar was a former slave who loved poetry and stories. She spent hours sharing them with her children. Paul Laurence Dunbar, her son, was only six years old when he began to recite poetry. As he was growing up, Paul Dunbar realized it was not easy being the only African American in his class in high school, but he worked hard and did well. With the help of his friends, Wilbur and Orville Wright, he published a newsletter, *The Dayton Tattler*.

Soon Dunbar was writing poems and short stories. His first book, *Oak and Ivy*, was published in 1892. Three years later, his second book, *Majors and Minors*, made him famous across the United States. Then he was invited to England, where his poems also became popular.

Much of Dunbar's work discussed life as an African American, but some of his poems were about topics that had nothing to do with race. Dunbar was the first African American to become known as a writer of both fiction and poetry. At the start of the twentieth century, he was one of the most popular poets in the country.

▶ Making America Laugh: James Thurber

When the United States was in serious economic trouble during the Great Depression of the 1930s, James Thurber

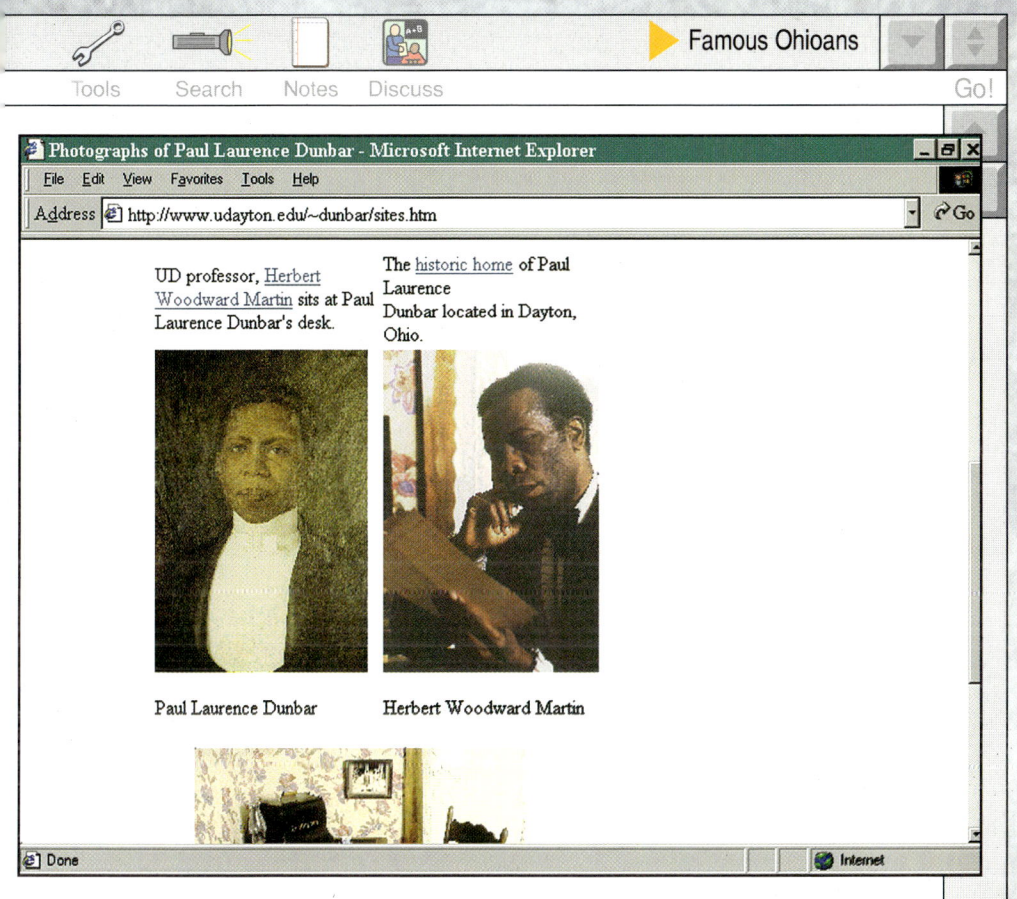

▲ Paul Laurence Dunbar was the first African American to become known as a writer of fiction and poetry.

made Americans laugh. His humor was not silly or corny. It was sophisticated and intelligent. It made people think as well as chuckle.

Born in Columbus, Thurber usually wrote about nervous, quiet men who were intimidated by their wives and uncomfortable in their jobs. Most of his stories first appeared in *The New Yorker*, a popular magazine. He also drew cartoons that featured tiny men, big wives, and misbehaving children.

▶ Modern Novelist

Toni Morrison is one of the most honored writers in the United States. In 1988, she won the Pulitzer Prize for

21

fiction for *Beloved*, the tragic story of a slave. Five years later, she became the first African-American woman to be awarded the Nobel Prize in Literature.

Morrison was born Chloe Anthony Wofford in Lorain, Ohio. She was the only African-American child in her first grade class, and the only student who could read.[1] After high school graduation, she left Ohio for college. She received degrees from Howard University and Cornell University. For years, she worked as a professor and an editor.

At night, while her children slept, Morrison began writing fiction. Her first novel, *The Bluest Eye*, was published in 1970. Since then, her books have been enjoyed by millions of readers.

▶ Into the Sky

Like their classmate, Paul Laurence Dunbar, Wilbur and Orville Wright grew up in Dayton. After graduating from high school, they went into business as printers. Then they opened a bicycle shop where they manufactured their own bikes.

In 1899, the Wright brothers became interested in gliders, or winged craft without power. They began experimenting with various types of wings and discovered that by curving the opposite tips in different ways, they could gain much control over their gliders.

After successful experiments near Kitty Hawk, North Carolina, the Wrights began working on a new aircraft back in their bicycle shop in Dayton. By adding a propeller, they turned their glider into a powered airplane.

On December 17, 1903, Orville made history by piloting the aircraft for twelve seconds over a distance of 120 feet at Kitty Hawk, North Carolina. The Wright brothers' plane had worked! In less than two years, they were

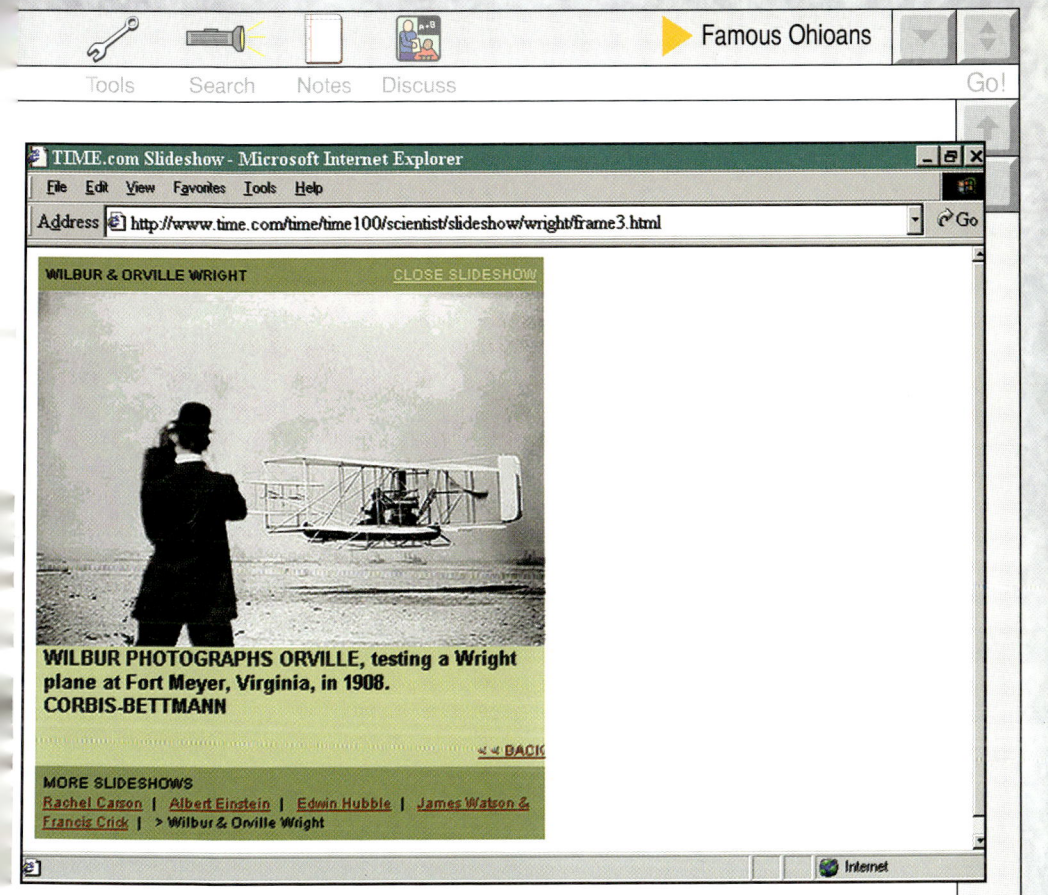

▲ The Wright brothers invented the first powered airplane. In this photograph, Wilbur is filming Orville as he tests a plane in Virginia in 1908.

flying 24.2 miles in thirty-eight minutes. Their invention was copied and soon was in use all over the world.

▶ Around the World

In 1962, the United States was ready to put a man in orbit around the earth. Colonel John H. Glenn, Jr., from New Concord, Ohio, was the astronaut chosen for the mission.

On February 20, Glenn's *Friendship 7* capsule orbited Earth three times in approximately ninety minutes. When he returned, Americans greeted him with parades and celebrations across the country. He was one of the most popular men in the world.

That great popularity helped Glenn after he retired from the space program. In 1974, he was elected as a U.S. senator from Ohio. Ten years later, he was a serious but unsuccessful candidate for president. Ohio voters reelected Glenn to the Senate three times.

In 1998, when he was seventy-seven years old, Glenn again captured the world's attention by returning to space. He had convinced officials that space would be a perfect setting in which to conduct experiments on the effects of old age. As America's oldest living former astronaut he argued that he would make a good subject to study. Glenn's flight aboard the Space Shuttle *Discovery* lasted nine days. The mission covered 3.6 million miles in 134 orbits.

On the Moon

The first man to walk on the moon was also an astronaut from Ohio. Neil A. Armstrong was the commander of *Apollo 11*. On July 20, 1969, he climbed down from his Eagle spacecraft and announced, "That's one small step for man, one giant leap for mankind."[2]

Armstrong had been a test pilot for years before becoming an astronaut. He flew more than two hundred types of jets, helicopters, and gliders. As the command pilot of *Gemini 8* in 1966, he performed the first docking of two vehicles in space.

The *Gemini 8* capsule now rests in the Neil Armstrong Air and Space Museum in Wapakoneta, Ohio. Wapakoneta is Armstrong's hometown.

The Harrisons

William Henry Harrison came to Ohio when he was a young man. He was elected to several political posts, but he became famous for fighting American Indians on the frontier. His efforts helped pave the way for the white settlement of Ohio. As a commander, Harrison led his soldiers to victories over Indian armies in 1811 at the Battle of Tippecanoe. Two years later, he defeated a coalition of American Indians led by Chief Tecumseh and their British allies in the Battle of the Thames in Canada.

In 1840, Harrison ran for president with John Tyler as his vice presidential candidate. Harrison and Tyler easily won the election, but the new president caught a cold at his inauguration. His condition gradually grew worse and he developed pneumonia.[3] He died on April 4, 1841, just one month after Inauguration Day. No other person has had such a short term. William Henry Harrison was the first president to die in office.

Forty-seven years later, another Harrison made a bid for the White House. Like his grandfather, Benjamin was a successful military leader who moved into politics. When he ran for president, his campaign song was "Grandfather's Hat Fits Ben." He received fewer popular votes than

Benjamin Harrison.

Grover Cleveland, his opponent. Still, Benjamin Harrison received a majority of electoral votes and became president in 1889. He served one term.

William Henry and Benjamin Harrison are the only grandfather and grandson to have both been elected president of the United States.

▶ Ohio's Streak

The Harrisons are not the only presidents with ties to Ohio. From 1868 to 1920, the United States elected twelve presidents—and seven of them were born in Ohio. Ulysses S. Grant moved to Illinois and became a Civil War hero. Rutherford B. Hayes, James A. Garfield, and William McKinley were Civil War soldiers who became Ohio politicians before moving to the White House. After being born at his grandfather's Ohio estate, Benjamin Harrison moved to Indiana. William Howard Taft and Warren G. Harding spent most of their lives in Ohio.

▶ The Strange Election

Rutherford B. Hayes, governor of Ohio, lost the popular vote in the election of 1876 by more than 250,000 votes to Samuel J. Tilden. It seemed like a clear-cut decision. The headlines read, "Tilden elected."[4]

It was not quite that simple. The electoral votes of three Southern states were in doubt. Without those disputed votes, Tilden led 184–165 in the electoral college. He needed one more electoral vote to become president. Congress created a commission to decide who would receive the disputed votes. Hayes's party, the Republicans, bargained with Southern politicians. They promised to remove all federal troops from the South, to put a Southern Democrat in the Cabinet, and to spend millions on building Southern railroads. Hayes wound up with all the disputed votes—and the presidency.

Despite the strange circumstances of his election, Hayes won respect as a hardworking, honest man during his single term in the White House.

▶ Death in the White House

William Henry Harrison was not the only president from Ohio who did not finish his term. James A. Garfield and William McKinley were both assassinated.

In 1880, the Republicans had difficulty deciding who to nominate for president. Finally, on the thirty-sixth ballot, they agreed on Garfield, a little-known representative from Ohio. He was elected a few months later.

After less than four months in the White House, Garfield was walking through a railroad station in Washington, D.C., when he was shot twice by a man with a pistol. For two months, doctors struggled to save the president. Eventually, his wounds became infected, and Garfield died on September 19, 1881.

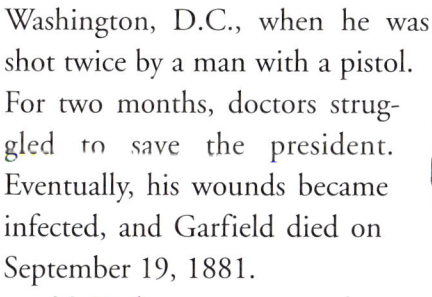

McKinley was a popular governor when he was elected president in

Rutherford B. ▶ Hayes.

1896. During his first term, the United States won the Spanish-American War, and in 1900 he was re-elected.

On September 6, 1901, McKinley attended a reception in Buffalo, New York. He met many people and shook hundreds of hands. One man used a handkerchief to hide a pistol in his hand. When the president approached expecting to shake another hand, the man shot him. McKinley died eight days later.

▶ The Biggest President

At more than three hundred pounds, William Howard Taft was America's heaviest president. Taft was a prosecuting attorney and a judge in Ohio before becoming secretary of war. In 1908, he was elected president. He did not enjoy the job and was overwhelmingly defeated when he ran for reelection.

As president, Taft had been in charge of the executive branch of government. In 1921, he became head of the judicial branch when President Warren G. Harding appointed him chief justice of the United States Supreme Court. It was a job Taft loved. For nine years, he worked hard to make the court function more efficiently. No other person has ever served both as president and chief justice.

▶ Scandal in the White House

Many historians have chosen Warren G. Harding as one of our least successful presidents. In 1920, he was a popular but largely ineffective U.S. senator from Ohio. He was not an ambitious man, but the Republicans needed a presidential candidate. When the convention could not agree on a nominee, they eventually settled on Harding.

After a clear victory in the election, Harding and many of his friends moved to Washington, D.C. Reporters called them "the Ohio Gang." The new president gave his friends important jobs in the government. Some of them were dishonest; they took bribes and stole government funds. Several of them later served time in prison.

Historians feel that Harding apparently did not know about the scandals. He died suddenly of pneumonia in 1923 before his friends were arrested.

▶ The First Woman Candidate

If Victoria Woodhull had had her way, Ohio would have been the home of the first woman president. When

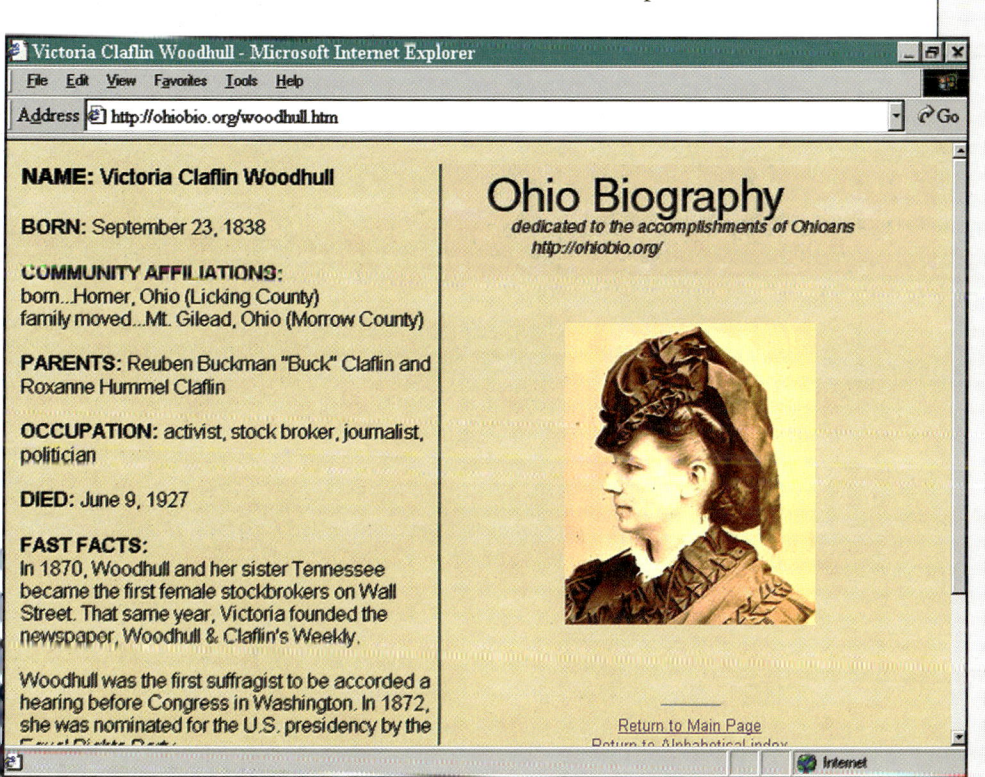

Ohio Biography
dedicated to the accomplishments of Ohioans
http://ohiobio.org/

NAME: Victoria Claflin Woodhull

BORN: September 23, 1838

COMMUNITY AFFILIATIONS:
born...Homer, Ohio (Licking County)
family moved...Mt. Gilead, Ohio (Morrow County)

PARENTS: Reuben Buckman "Buck" Claflin and Roxanne Hummel Claflin

OCCUPATION: activist, stock broker, journalist, politician

DIED: June 9, 1927

FAST FACTS:
In 1870, Woodhull and her sister Tennessee became the first female stockbrokers on Wall Street. That same year, Victoria founded the newspaper, Woodhull & Claflin's Weekly.

Woodhull was the first suffragist to be accorded a hearing before Congress in Washington. In 1872, she was nominated for the U.S. presidency by the

▲ Victoria Woodhull was the first woman to run for president.

Woodhull was born in 1838 in Homer, Ohio, American women could not vote. Few women graduated from, or even attended, high school. Almost all highly paid professional jobs were held by men.

Woodhull was not interested in a quiet life in Ohio. Despite having little formal education, she moved to New York City with her sister, Tennessee Claflin. Together they became the first independent female American stockbrokers. Newspapers called them "The Queens of Finance." They also produced a popular newspaper, *Woodhull and Claflin's Weekly*.

Woodhull was probably one of the most famous women in the country when she was nominated for president by the Equal Rights Party in 1872. She was the first woman to attempt to win the White House. She met with little success, but her efforts helped pave the way for the great progress American women made in the twentieth century.

▶ Track-and-Field Superstar

Jesse Owens was one of the greatest athletes who ever lived. When he was an eighth grader growing up in Cleveland, Ohio, he ran the 100-yard dash in 9.9 seconds. By the time he was a senior in high school, he had cut half a second off his time to tie the world record.

As an member of the Ohio State University track team, he set world records in the long jump, 220-yard dash, 200-meter dash, 220-yard low hurdles, and 200-meter hurdles on May 25, 1935. All in less than an hour.

Owens, an African American, took four gold medals at the Olympics in Berlin, Germany, in 1936. His incredible performance was a severe embarrassment to Nazi leader Adolf Hitler, who had proclaimed that Aryans were the superior race.

Leader of the Buckeyes

For years, Woody Hayes was one of the most successful college football coaches in the United States. His teams at Ohio State University won national titles in 1954, 1957, and 1968. The Buckeye fans loved him.

Hayes was not as popular outside of Ohio. He was as famous for his temper tantrums on the field and in the locker room as he was for his great teams. It was not unusual for him to rip off his cap and tear it to pieces. Once he bloodied himself by crushing his eyeglasses in his bare hands. He was also known to punch himself in the face. He said, "The minute I think I'm getting mellow, I'm retiring. Who ever heard of a mellow winner?"[5]

For the most part, the people of Ohio forgave Hayes for his tantrums. They remembered his championships and the way he cared for his players, sometimes long after they had finished their careers. In twenty-eight seasons, his teams won 205 games.

The Golden Bear

For decades the dominant golfer in the world was Jack Nicklaus, a quiet man from Columbus. In fact, until Tiger Woods came on the scene, most experts picked Nicklaus as the greatest golfer of all time.

When he began his career, he was a big, heavy man with blond hair. His fans nicknamed him the "Golden Bear." Later he lost weight, but the victories kept coming.

Nicklaus was the first man to win all of golf's major titles twice. These are the U.S. Open, British Open, Masters Tournament, and PGA (Professional Golfers Association) Tournament.

Chapter 4

Government and Economy

In Ohio, any town with more than five thousand people is classified as a city. If it is smaller, it is a village. Most of the cities are run by councils or commissions.

In 1913, Dayton became the first large American city to be run by an appointed city manager. Since then, that idea has spread throughout the nation. Ohio is divided into eighty-eight counties. They are each governed by councils or boards.

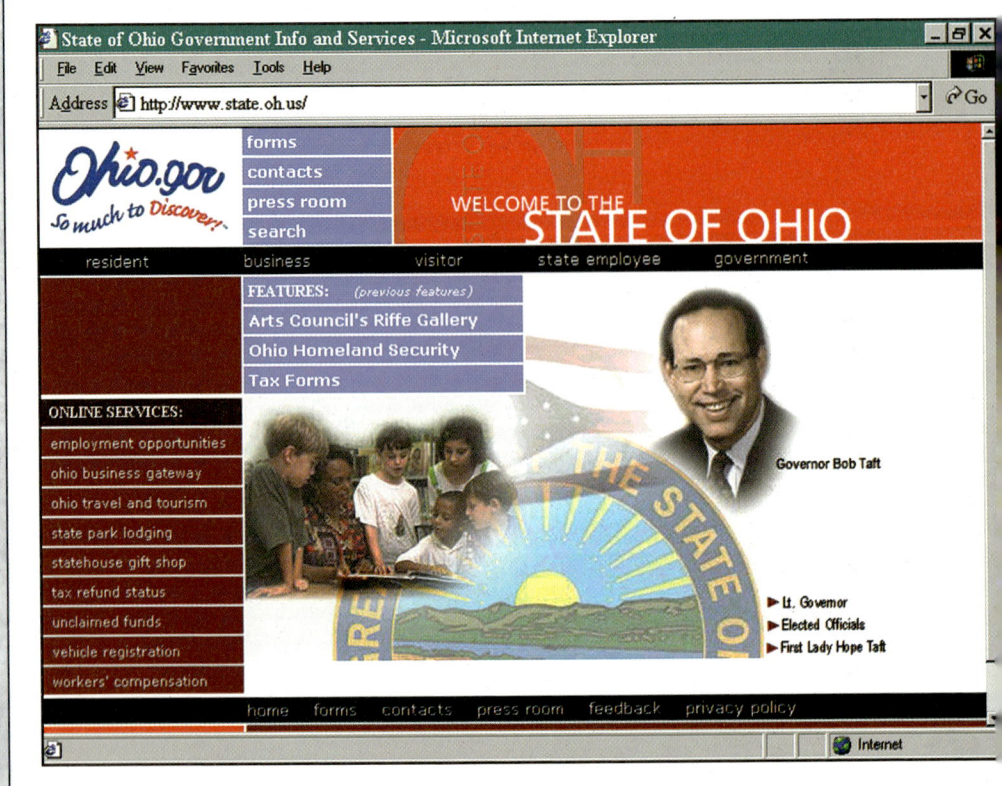

▲ *Bob Taft was elected governor of Ohio in 1999.*

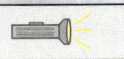

▶ Running the State

The state government has three branches—legislative, judicial, and executive. The state legislature, or lawmaking body, meets in the capitol building in Columbus. It is made up of thirty-three members in the state senate and ninety-nine members in the state house of representatives.

The state supreme court, with seven justices, also meets in Columbus and heads Ohio's judicial branch. It presides over a system of courts of appeals and common pleas. There are also county, juvenile, and probate courts.

The chief executive officer is the governor. He or she appoints the heads of most state agencies and departments.

Taxes pay for most of the state government's services. About a third of the budget is funded by a personal income tax. Residents also pay special taxes on gasoline, cigarettes, and liquor. A state lottery brings in millions of dollars annually.

▶ Making Money

Ohio is one of the most important manufacturing states. One-fourth of the country's trucks are made in Ohio. No other state makes more household appliances. Ohio produces much of the nation's steel and aluminum. The state's factories also produce billions of dollars worth of cars, buses, cash registers, airplane parts, and construction equipment.

Mining is an important part of Ohio's economy as well. The state produces rock salt, limestone, coal, and sandstone.

Farming also generates revenue. For almost two hundred years, corn has been Ohio's most important crop. Wheat, soybeans, milk, and hay are also cash crops.

Most of the state's workers are employed in service

▲ *The Ohio statehouse in Columbus.*

industries. They work for government agencies, banks, hospitals, hotels, and stores.

▶ The People

According to the 2000 U.S. census, there are 11,353,140 people living in Ohio. Most of them were born in the United States. Their ancestors came largely from England, Germany, Ireland, and other European countries.

About 11.5 percent of the population is African American. Approximately 1.9 percent is Hispanic American.

Only about a fourth of Ohio's population lives in small towns or in the country. The rest live in urban areas. About two-fifths of the people live in the state's three largest metropolitan areas—Columbus, Cleveland, and Cincinnati.

Chapter 5

History

Not much is known about the first people who lived in Ohio. These Paleo-Americans hunted and gathered nuts and fruit. They disappeared before the arrival of those called American Indians. The only artifacts they left were arrowheads and knives.

▶ American Indians

The Mound Builders arrived about two thousand years ago. Besides hunting and gathering, they also did a little farming. They left behind pottery, weapons, pipes, decorations, and thousands of mounds.

The Adena Indians were responsible for the Great Serpent Mound. It is so big it can really only be seen and appreciated from the air. Nobody really knows the purpose of this giant mound shaped like an animal.

The Hopewell Indians, the last of the Mound Builders, occupied the area until about A.D. 500. They had a highly developed civilization. Besides making beautiful artwork, they also traded with other groups throughout North America. Shells from the Caribbean and rocks from the Rocky Mountains were found in their tombs. After the Mound Builders faded away, other tribes moved in. Early in the 1700s, Iroquois Indians controlled most of the land that became Ohio.

▶ The Whites Come

René-Robert Cavelier, Sieur de La Salle, was most likely the first European to visit the Ohio Valley. He was a

Serpent Mound

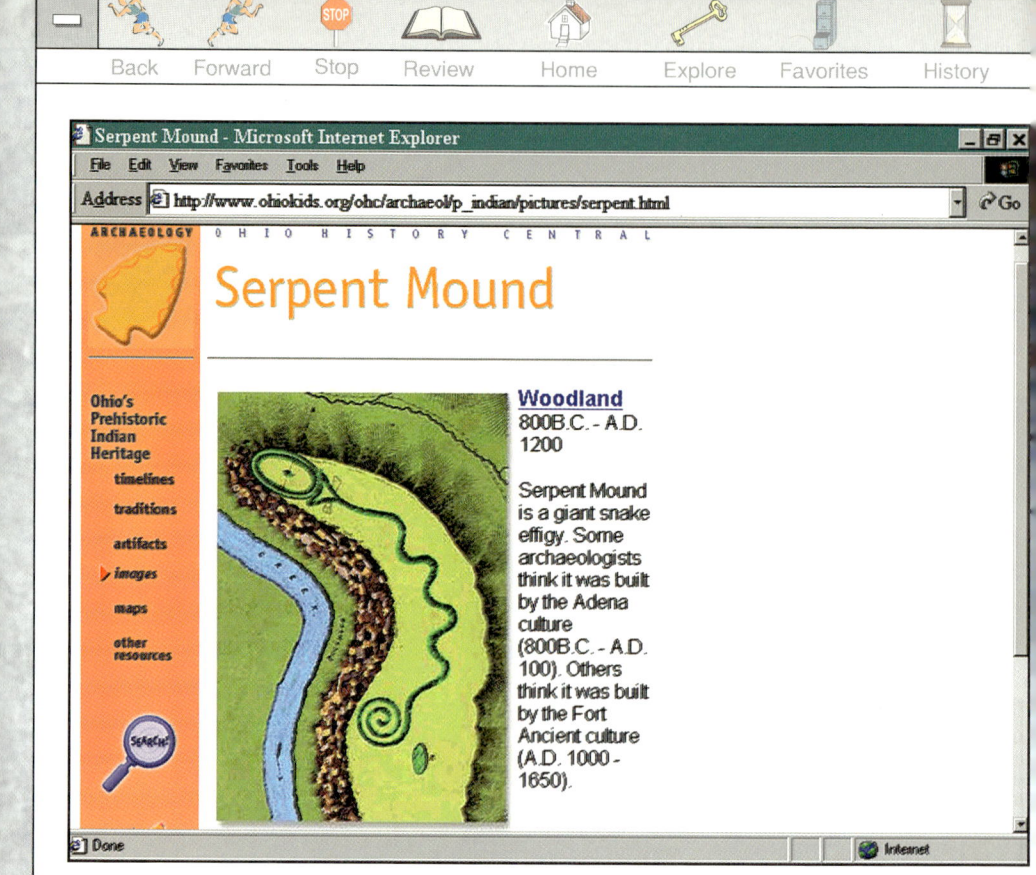

Woodland
800 B.C. - A.D. 1200

Serpent Mound is a giant snake effigy. Some archaeologists think it was built by the Adena culture (800 B.C. - A.D. 100). Others think it was built by the Fort Ancient culture (A.D. 1000 - 1650).

▲ *It is believed that the Adena Indians are responsible for building the mysterious Great Serpent Mound.*

Frenchman who explored the entire Great Lakes region. He probably arrived in Ohio around 1670. Due to La Salle's explorations, France claimed most of the middle of the North American continent.

The British established colonies on the Atlantic coast and claimed all the land extending west through the territory claimed by the French. The dispute over the Ohio Valley was one of the causes of the French and Indian War (1754–63), fought between Britain and France and their American Indian allies.

When France lost the war, it gave up all claims to Ohio in the Peace of Paris of 1763. After the American Revolution, the land belonged to the United States.

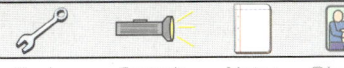

Trouble between Natives and Settlers

American Indians did not want to see white settlers move to their land. Pontiac, an Iroquois chieftain, continued to lead his Indian warriors against the British even after the French left. During the Revolutionary War, the British promised to stop new white settlement. Thus, the Shawnee fought against the Americans.

When the British left after the successful American Revolution, Americans in great numbers began coming to Ohio. Marietta was the first permanent white settlement. Many Revolutionary War veterans were given land in Ohio as a reward for their service.

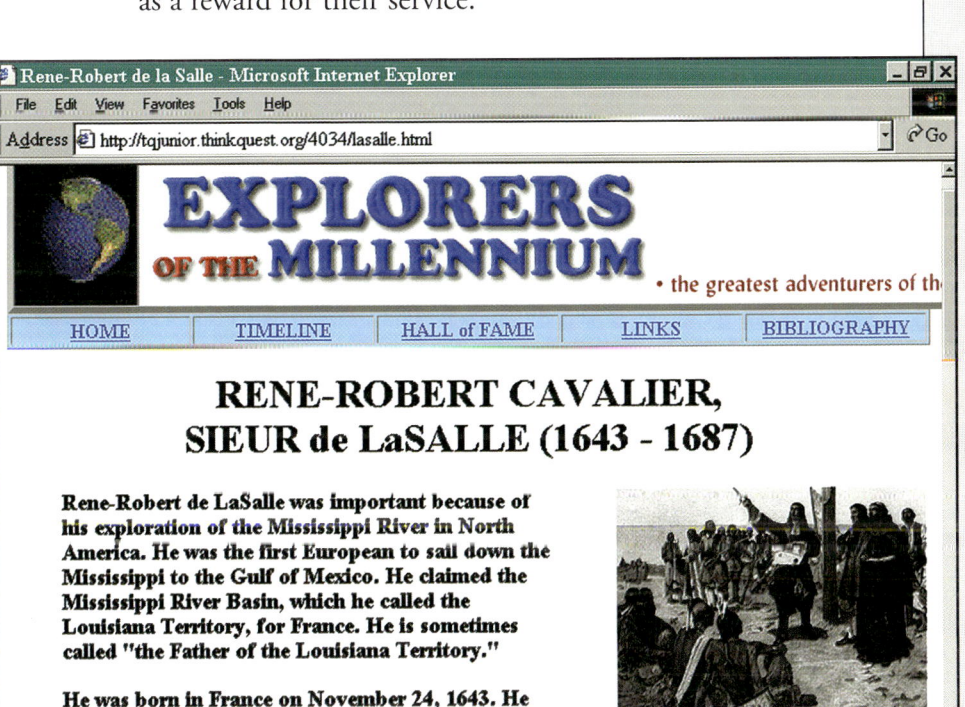

▲ René-Robert Cavelier, Sieur de La Salle, is most likely the first European to have visited the Ohio Valley.

The natives resented the growing white presence on their land. Chief Little Turtle of the Miami people organized several raids against the settlers. When General Anthony Wayne defeated him at the Battle of Fallen Timbers, the American Indians lost control of Ohio. In 1795, American Indian chiefs signed the Treaty of Greenville, which gave most of their land to the United States.

▶ Statehood

Americans poured into Ohio when the American Indian uprisings ended. By 1803, almost seventy thousand of them lived there. That year Ohio became the seventeenth state in the United States.

The first state capital was in Chillicothe. Soon, the state offices were moved once and for all to Columbus. The citizens of Ohio wanted the capital located in the middle of their state. Columbus has been the capital since 1816.

▶ A Real War—and a Fake One

During the War of 1812, the United States again battled Britain. Ohio was the scene of an important battle. Oliver Hazard Perry brought nine small American ships to Put-in-Bay, Ohio, on the coast of Lake Erie. Perry's fleet met six larger British ships on September 10, 1813.

When Perry's ship, the USS *Lawrence*, was hit and disabled, he jumped into a rowboat and boarded another American ship and continued the fight. When two British ships became entangled, the Americans pounded them with cannon fire.

Soon the British surrendered. Perry sent a famous message, "We have met the enemy and they are ours."[1] After that, American forces controlled all of Lake Erie.

In 1835, Ohio was involved in another dispute, this time with other Americans. As more and more settlers arrived, the territory of Michigan, north of Ohio, was preparing to become a state. Michigan and Ohio, though, could not agree on their border. Both sides argued Toledo was on their side of the line.

The states threatened to fight for the strip of land. President Andrew Jackson did not want a civil war to erupt, so he told the two sides to compromise. When Stevens Mason, Michigan's territorial governor, refused to give in, Jackson fired him.

Finally an agreement was reached. Ohio received the Toledo strip, but Michigan was given its upper peninsula, nine thousand miles of mostly unsettled land. The "Toledo War" was over.[2]

▶ Using the Waterways

It was not easy for farmers on the western side of the new state to transport their produce to the big cities in the east. It was a long, difficult trip over the Appalachian Mountains.

This changed with the Louisiana Purchase in 1803. Now the middle of the continent belonged to the United States. Most important for the people of Ohio, the Port of New Orleans was opened to Americans. That

▲ *Before the railroad was built in Ohio, steamboats transported goods from Ohio to New Orleans, Louisiana.*

meant farmers could load their goods on boats that could travel down the Ohio River to the Mississippi River to New Orleans. From there, the boats made their way through the Gulf of Mexico to the Atlantic Ocean and to big cities on the East Coast.

Steamboats, whose powerful wheels could easily take them up and down the rivers, were soon a familiar sight on the Ohio and Mississippi.

Farmers who did not live close to the Ohio River still had to transport their goods long distances over land. To solve that problem, Alfred Kelley, a lawyer in Cleveland, designed a system of canals. Beginning in 1825, crews began digging the canals, which were narrow man-made rivers. Small flatboats were pulled along by mules that walked on trails beside the water. Travel was slow, but much easier than trying to go over land.

The Ohio and Erie Canal stretched from the Ohio River to Cleveland on Lake Erie. It was finished in 1832. Thirteen years later, the Miami and Erie Canal connected Toledo and Cincinnati. Now it was much easier for farmers throughout the state to get their goods to the major waterways and then to the country's big cities.

▶ Railroads Come to Ohio

It was difficult to dig Ohio's canals without power machinery. Most of the work had to be done with shovels. After all that effort, the canals were only in use for about twenty-five years.

Railroads changed everything. A charging locomotive can travel much faster than a flatboat being pulled by a mule, or even a big steamboat with its powerful paddle wheel. A train also can carry much more cargo than a small boat on a narrow canal. There was no longer a need to transport crops all the way to New Orleans and then around Florida to reach the East Coast.

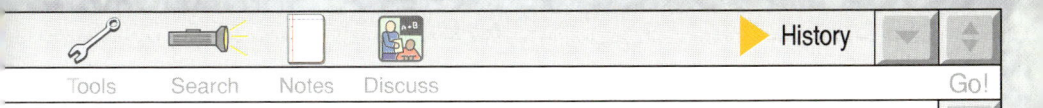

Soon Ohio was sending tons of lumber and farm products to America's big cities. Before the Civil War, Ohio's farms were producing and selling more wheat and corn than any other state.

With the railroads bringing in raw materials and carrying out finished products, factories and mills were now being built along tracks throughout Ohio. Thousands of people moved to the state to take jobs in the cities or to start farms in the country. By 1850, Ohio had more people than all but two of the other states.

▲ The railroad increased greatly Ohio's production and industrial centers, because goods could be transported more easily. As a result, more people began moving to Ohio to take advantage of the new jobs.

Civil War and Growth

Slavery was never allowed in Ohio. The first state constitution in 1803 prohibited it. Most people in the state were also opposed to slavery. They supported the efforts of the Underground Railroad, which brought escaped slaves from the South through Ohio and into freedom in Canada.

Uncle Tom's Cabin

One of the main causes of the Civil War was the differing lifestyles between the people of the North and the South. Especially the use of slavery in the Southern states. No one did more to stir up antislavery feelings in the North than Harriet Beecher Stowe.

When she lived in Ohio, Stowe came into contact with the Underground Railroad that assisted slaves by sneaking them out of the South. She heard stories about the terrible abuse that slaves suffered at the hands of their masters.

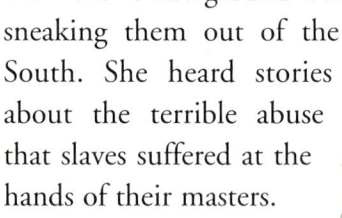

Stowe used this information when she wrote *Uncle Tom's Cabin*, a powerful antislavery novel published in 1852. It

Harriet Beecher Stowe.

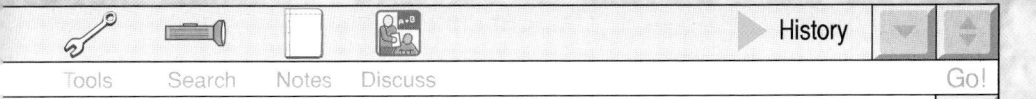

told the story of slaves abused by a cruel overseer, Simon Legree. *Uncle Tom's Cabin* was later transformed into a play, which was produced all across the Northern states.

Northern readers and audiences were infuriated by the book and the play. They figured that if slaveholders were that mean, something had to be done. Southerners were also angered. They felt that the book greatly exaggerated the cruelty, and that most slaves were not treated that badly.[3]

About 345,000 troops from Ohio fought for the Union during the Civil War. Still, not everybody in the state supported President Abraham Lincoln and the Union. Thousands of Ohio residents in the southern part of the state sympathized with the South. Their leader was Clement L. Vallandigham, of Dayton. He and his followers were known as Peace Democrats, or Copperheads.

As the tide swung in favor of the North, support for the Copperheads eroded. The Union won the war in 1865 and slavery was soon abolished.

After the war, hundreds of factories were built in Ohio, most of them in the larger cities. Lake Erie became a water highway for shipping large amounts of heavy products such as coal and iron ore. Ohio's coastal cities—Cleveland, Sandusky, and Lorain—became important ports.

John D. Rockefeller founded the Standard Oil Company in Cleveland. He became one of the world's richest men, and his company one of America's largest. Proctor and Gamble, a significant maker of household cleaning products, built its headquarters in Cincinnati. Steel mills made Youngstown a major manufacturing city. The new automobile industry needed millions of tires, which the rubber factories of Akron helped supply.

▲ *Recently, the state of Ohio has begun to rebuild and clean up the city of Cleveland, pictured here. The state hopes this project will make the city more attractive and attract more tourists.*

▶ Death at Kent State University

Americans were deeply divided by the Vietnam War in the 1960s and 1970s. More than 600,000 American troops were sent to the tiny Southeast Asian country to fight against Communist soldiers. Many Americans felt the war was a worthwhile fight for liberty. Others thought it was a foolish waste of materials and lives. Many of the war's opponents were college students.

When President Richard Nixon expanded the war in 1970 with extensive bombing in the nearby country of Cambodia, protests erupted around the country. At Kent State University in Kent, protests turned into riots as buildings were burned. The Ohio National Guard was called out.

On May 4, the guardsmen fired into a crowd of unarmed protesters. Four of them were killed.

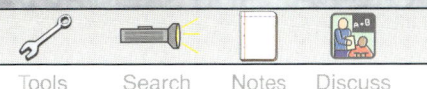

Photographs of the dying students appeared in newspapers around the world.

Modern Problems

For decades, factories, businesses, and homes simply dumped their waste products into rivers. It seemed like an easy way to get rid of what was no longer needed. The resulting pollution killed fish and plants. It also made the water dirty and foul-smelling. In 1969, the Cuyahoga River was so filled with oil that it actually caught fire.

The state and national governments began efforts to clean up Ohio's water. New laws controlled the dumping of wastes. Slowly, the condition of the rivers and lakes began to improve.

As more people moved out of big cities into nearby suburbs, Cleveland, Toledo, Columbus, and Cincinnati suffered. Stores and businesses in the central cities closed. The governments collected less tax money.

Urban Renewal

To counter the problem, the cities tried to come up with rebuilding programs to make them more attractive to tourists, businesses, and potential homeowners. One of the most successful urban renewal projects has been in Cleveland. Instead of empty buildings, the city's lakefront now boasts such attractions as Jacobs Field and the Rock and Roll Hall of Fame and Museum.

Even with the problems that it may have, many people continue to choose to live in Ohio. It remains one of the most important industrial states, and as of the 2000 U.S. census, ranked seventh in total population. In addition, tourists from all over flock to places such as the Cleveland waterfront to spend their vacations.

Chapter Notes

Ohio Facts

1. *USA State Symbols, Flags & Facts*, CD-ROM, Toronto: Canada: Robesus, Inc., 2001.

2. Ibid.

Chapter 3. Famous Ohioans

1. "Toni Morrison," *History Channel Exhibits: Black History Month*, 2002, <http://www.historychannel.com/exhibits/blacklist/0226.html> (May 9, 2002).

2. Catherine Watson, "The Apollo 11 Mission," *NASA Human Spaceflight History*, August 30, 2001, <http://spaceflight.nasa.gov/history/apollo/apollo11/> (May 21, 2002).

3. William A. DeGregorio, *The Complete Book of U.S. Presidents* (New York: Dembner Books, 1984), p. 145.

4. "February 5, 1877: The Florida Case," *Series of "Historical Minutes," 1868–1913*, n.d., <http://www.senate.gov/learning/min_4bb.html> (May 8, 2002).

5. Alex Fineman, "Hayes Produced Champions, Controversy," *Sportscentury Biography*, 2002, <http://espn.go.com/classic/biography/s/Hayes_Woody.html> (May 8, 2002).

Chapter 5. History

1. Allan R. Millett and Peter Maslowski, *For the Common Defense* (New York: The Free Press, 1994), p. 112.

2. C. M. Davis, "The Toledo War," *Michigan State University Department of Geography*, n.d., <http://www.geo.msu.edu/geo333/toledo_war.html> (May 8, 2002).

3. Mary Beth Norton, et. al., *A People and a Nation: A History of the United States*, vol. 1, (Boston: Houghton Mifflin Company, 1990), p. 380.

Further Reading

Boekhoff, P. M. and Stuart A. Kallen. *Ohio*. Farmington Hills, Mich.: Gale Group, 2002.

Burke, James Lee and Kenneth E. Davison. *Ohio's Heritage*. Layton, Utah: Smith, Gibbs Publisher, 1984.

Georgiady, Nicholas P. and Louis G. Romano. *Ohio First Settlers: The Indians–Native Americans*. Second ed. Okemos, Mich.: Argee Publishers, 1995.

———. *Ohio Women*. Second ed. Okemos, Mich.: Argee Publishers, 1995.

Heinrichs, Ann. *Ohio*. Danbury, Conn.: Children's Press, 1999.

Joseph, Paul. *Ohio*. Edina, Minn.: ABDO Pub Company, 1998.

Marsh, Carole. *Ohio History!: Surprising Secrets About Our State's Founding Mothers, Fathers, and Kids!*. Peachtree City, Ga.: Gallopade International, 1996.

Martin, Michael A. *Ohio: The Buckeye State*. Milwaukee, Wis.: Gareth Stevens, Inc., 2002.

Sherrow, Victoria. *Ohio*. Tarrytown, N.Y.: Marshall Cavendish Corporation, 1998.

Sowash, Rick. *Heroes of Ohio: 23 True Tales of Courage & Character*. Bowling Green, Ohio: Gabriel's Horn Publishing Company, Inc., 1998.

Wills, Charles A. *A Historical Album of Ohio*. Brookfield, Ohio: Millbrook Press, Inc., 1996.

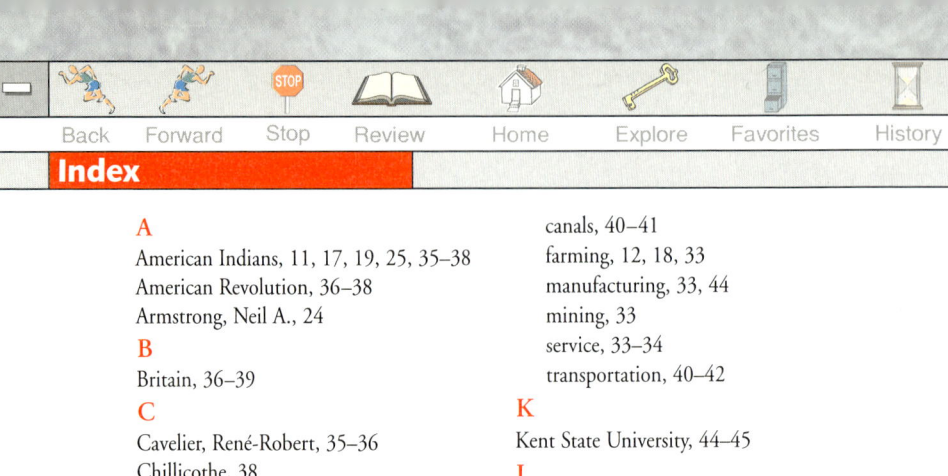

Index

A
American Indians, 11, 17, 19, 25, 35–38
American Revolution, 36–38
Armstrong, Neil A., 24

B
Britain, 36–39

C
Cavalier, René-Robert, 35–36
Chillicothe, 38
Cincinnati, 12, 15, 40, 44–45
Civil War, 41–43
Cleveland, 12, 14–15, 18, 45
climate, 16–17
Columbus, 12, 17–18, 21, 33–34, 38, 45
Copperheads, 43–44

D
Dayton, 13, 18, 22, 32
Dunbar, Paul Laurence, 20, 22

E
economy, 33–34
education, 11, 17

F
France, 36–37
French and Indian War, 36

G
gained statehood, 11
Garfield James A., 26–27
geography,
    caves, 19
    glaciers, 16–17
    hills, 11, 16–17
    lakes, 17–18, 38, 40, 44
    rivers, 11, 17–18, 40
Glenn, Jr., John H., 23–24
Grant, Ulysses S., 26
Great Serpent Mound, 19, 35
Greenville, Treaty of, 38

H
Harding, Warren G., 26, 28–29
Harrison, Benjamin, 25–26
Harrison, William Henry, 24–27
Hayes, Rutherford B., 26–27
Hayes, Woody, 31
history, 12, 20, 35–45

I
industry,
    canals, 40–41
    farming, 12, 18, 33
    manufacturing, 33, 44
    mining, 33
    service, 33–34
    transportation, 40–42

K
Kent State University, 44–45

L
Lake Erie, 17–18, 38, 40, 44

M
Mason, Stevens, 39
McKinley, William, 26–28
Morrison, Toni, 21–22

N
Nicklaus, Jack, 31

O
Ohio Gang, 29
Ohio River, 11, 17–18, 40,
Owens, Jesse, 30

P
Perry, Oliver Hazard, 38–39
population, 34, 45

R
recreation,
    amusement parks, 15, 18
    museums, 13–14, 24, 45
    sports, 12–13, 45
    zoos, 14–15

S
state government, 32–33
Stowe, Harriet Beecher, 42

T
Taft, William Howard, 28
Thurber, James, 20–21
Toledo, 14, 18, 39–40, 45
Toledo War, 39

V
Vallandigham, Clement L., 43

W
War of 1812, 38–39
Wayne, Anthony, 38
Woodhull, Victoria, 29–30
Wright brothers, 20, 22–23

977.1 K727o
Knapp, Ron.
Ohio

1096164536   MAR 25 2003